TABLE OF CONTENTS

I0409923

i

Chapter 1
Introduction

"In the ten years following World War II, however, Congress was almost constantly occupied with major substantive issues of military policy: selective service, universal military training, the size of the active forces, the composition of the reserve forces, the organization of the defense establishment, the conditions of service for officers and enlisted men."[1]
Samuel P. Huntington, The Soldier and the State

More than a decade has passed since the end of the Cold War, yet despite the swirling winds of "revolution" and the constant prodding of Congress, the United States military (and many would argue, the entire Department of Defense) of the new millennium looks much like its old self. Despite, or maybe as a result of, the military's attempts to employ a transformation strategy, the U.S. has instead witnessed an increasing level of bureaucracy, marked by an increasing number of staffs and department agencies, which threaten to erode mission effectiveness. The products of the Quadrennial Defense Review (QDR), National Defense Panel (NDP), and Defense Reform Initiative (DRI) have yet to take root in their efforts to foster the realization of the Chairman of the Joint Chiefs of Staff's *Joint Vision 2010.*[2] Is the Army National Guard infrastructure currently in place robust and flexible enough to serve our nation's needs in the future or is it time to reform in order to shape it for the Twenty First Century?

Throughout most of its short history, the United States has maintained a small regular army in peacetime, backed up by some form of a reserve force.[3] Both have gone through cycles of neglect and diminished preparedness in periods of lessened danger and

1

upon demobilization after a war. The significance of threats to national security, time available to mobilize, proximity of the area of conflict, capabilities and ranges of weaponry, a cultural-political disinclination for a standing army, and belief in the concept of the citizen-soldier are among the factors contributing to poor peacetime military preparedness. At the conclusion of each of the major military conflicts involving the United States, the nation was anxious to demobilize and return to the status quo of a small active duty force backed up by a reserve component that in practice was not adequately resourced to be prepared for war.[4] However, the risks, in light of the international environment, were acceptable. From a historical viewpoint, the National Guard has made important contributions to the success of the United States in wartime.[5]

After the collapse of the Soviet Union, the U. S. military found itself as the world's only superpower and the Department of Defense soon realized that it could no longer sustain its current infrastructure. It also had a compelling reason to shift away from a strategy of containment. The United States codified a new National Military Strategy in 1997 that was embodied by the terms "Shape, Respond and Prepare Now."[6] This document portrays the grand strategy of the United States as a combination of cooperative security and selective engagement with an underlying theme of primacy. The national strategy has prompted some to refer to the United Stated as a "benevolent hegemon."[7] Riding the crest of the technological revolution and galvanized by the ideals put forward by General John Shalikashvili of *Joint Vision 2010*[8], leaders within each service looked ahead at the roadmaps of their respective services. The Army's approach to these changes was the concept of the Interim Brigade Combat Team (IBCT), as a step to a final Objective Force.[9] This vision emphasized rapidly deployable combat units, capable of self-sustainment and the ability to proceed directly into operations without the normal lengthy build-up period normally experienced by Army units in the past. This would significantly compress the usual amount of time associated with the call-up and train-up of National Guard units prior to their deployment/employment.

In the past, the National Guard has sought to fulfill two missions that at times has been hard to balance. The first is to serve as the primary combat reserve of the Army, and the second to fulfill a peacetime state mission of ensuring public safety, protecting property, and maintaining public order.[10] Even with the transformation of active duty forces, they will continue to require augmentation for combat support and combat service support units that can arguably be better sustained by the National Guard units. These units possess the types of skills and assets more useful in meeting emergency management, disaster response, and severe civil disorder (EM/DR/SCD)[11], rather than manning traditional combat systems like tanks, armored personnel carriers and howitzers. In addition, the post Cold War draw-down and dispersion among the states of Guard assets make it increasingly unlikely that a governor will have the kind of assets needed to meet their internal requirements organic within their state's units.

Simultaneously, throughout the 1990's, preparedness for and response to natural disasters have become high-priority for all levels of government. Catastrophic disasters, such as Hurricane Andrew in 1992, illustrate the need for rapid, coordinated, and efficient interagency response, including the National Guard. In a 1993 report, the General Accounting Office addressed the relationship between preparedness for national security emergencies and domestic civil emergency preparedness and response.[12]

3

Concerning the National Guard, the report said, "[The Department of Defense], the state guard units, and the governors must devote more attention to the need for a more extensive role for state guards in emergency management, particularly disaster response. Until some new balance is struck between missions and capabilities…the pressure to call for federal troops in the event of disasters or civil disorder will continue, or even grow."[13]

The Army must balance its fundamental military traditions and policies with the new realities of the new millennium. This means being very pragmatic about active duty and National Guard roles. But as with most crucial decisions, time is of the essence. The Army policy[14] of today represents the evolution of our Founding Fathers' vision to ensure a balance between federal and state governments. A review and validation of these thoughts are in order to maintain this delicate and proper balance. This dilemma calls for a radical solution. By declaring the National Guard be primarily responsible for the homeland defense of the United States and thereby, by default, focusing the active duty forces on external defense, the Army would be clarifying the roles of each. Homeland defense would include the ability to respond to emergency management, disaster response, and severe civil disorder (EM/DR/SCD).[15] In a well-articulated policy, the National Guard could have the lead in the domestic arena supported by the active Army.[16] In the foreign arena, active forces could be supported by those of the Guard. Such a clearly defined division of labor would provide adequate missions for all components and facilitate establishing training and resourcing priorities for all. America's Army could finally speak with one voice.

The purpose of this study is to determine the proper role of the National Guard in preparing for and responding to national disasters and domestic emergencies. It will also explore the feasibility of utilizing these types of forces in military operations other than war (MOOTW) missions to enable the active duty units to focus and train for major theater wars in the future. The time has come for the U.S. Army to consider the possibility of fielding a restructured, reorganized, and more relevant and useful Army National Guard now.

Chapter 2

<u>Historical Background</u>

"To provide for organizing, arming, and disciplining, the Militia, and for governing such Part of them as may be employed in the Service of the United States, reserving to the States respectively, the Appointment of the Officers, and the Authority of training the Militia according to the discipline prescribed by Congress;"[17]

U. S. Constitution

The citizen-soldier, as an extension of English tradition, was a natural component of the social structure of the original American colonies when they were first established. These citizen-soldiers, known as the militia, were organized on a local basis by the individual colonies to provide security and protect property. The structure of the colonial militia was highlighted by local recruitment, which included the election of officers, short periods of duty to meet immediate threats and restrictions of service to within colonial boundaries. The militia included all able-bodied men who were, through tradition, morally and legally obligated to defend the colony.[18] As the populations of the colonies expanded, local regimental organizations were established.

During the French and Indian War in the mid-eighteenth century, the English recruited provisional volunteer regiments from the colonies. Receiving training and leadership from English officers, these provisional units were more effective than the strictly local militia. Several of the colonies made these provisional regiments a permanent part of their militia. The oldest colonial regiments were Massachusetts' North, South and East Regiments. Today, the 101st Engineer Battalion; 1st Battalion, 181st Infantry Regiment; 1st Battalion, 182nd Infantry Regiment; and the 101st Field Artillery Battalion, all of the Massachusetts Army National Guard, trace their roots to these original militia regiments. These are the oldest units in the U.S. Army today.[19]

In the Revolutionary War period from 1775 to 1783 the militia played a vital role in securing independence from Great Britain. The idea of a continental army mustered from the several colonies for the duration of the war was beyond the political, economic and logistical wherewithal of the Continental Congress to impose on the colonies. Although the requirements for militia service were relatively clear, the realities for the militia were different. The militia exhibited poor discipline, training and organization. In most colonies (and then states), there was little or no compliance with the mandated universal military service obligation.[20]

However, in the early nineteenth century, a new type of militia arose. These were units composed not of men legally obligated to serve, but of volunteers. These units often wore colorful uniforms, trained and performed muster and were among the best prepared for federal service. In general though, the century following the Revolutionary War, saw the United States continue further into a period of anti-military sentiment regarding large standing armies and relative political-military isolation. European ambitions were neutralized and no immediate external threats foreseen. The wars the United States did get involved in (War of 1812, Indian, Mexican, Spanish), were met with federal forces in being, federal volunteers, militia volunteers and untrained militia called to active duty for short periods, sometimes for only one to three months.[21] From these early volunteer beginnings of militia service would emerge today's Army National Guard.

During the Civil War, the various state militias gave their allegiances to their respective states and answered the call to arms to serve in the Union or Confederate

Armies. The official records of the U.S. Army indicate the militia rolls had 3,200,000 personnel (2,500,000 in the United States and 700,000 in the Confederate States).[22] These figures did not reflect the almost total lack of training of individual militia, not a surprising situation in an era of relative isolation from any outside threat. The Militia Act of 1792 was the legal basis for the first call-up of 75,000 militia personnel in 1861 to serve for three months in the Union Army.[23] Approximately 2.7 million men would eventually serve in the Union Army between 1861 and 1865, of which 1.9 million were from state militia (recognizing that many individuals served multiple terms of enlistment).[24] The Confederate Army mustered about a million men from the southern states throughout the war. The first call-up from the state militia was for 100,000 troops for one year of service.[25] Like the North, the Confederate Army was to be principally composed of volunteers from the militia.[26]

As the nineteenth century concluded, the United States completed over a hundred years without the need for a large standing army or federal reserve force. However, its position of geographic isolation and insulation from European wars ended as the American industrial revolution and the global nature of conflict thrust the country into the role of a major world power with international responsibilities. The Spanish-American War, from 21 April 1898 to 12 August 1898, involved 173,000 volunteers from the militia to meet the manpower requirements of the nation.[27] These troops were involved in the campaigns to secure Puerto Rico and Santiago, Cuba. Volunteers also formed the major portion (seventy-five per cent of initial troops) of the force that deployed to the Philippines.[28]

Early into the Twentieth Century, The National Defense Act of 1903, or Dick Act (named after the congressman and militia Major General from Ohio), replaced the Militia Act of 1792 (which had mandated service in the militia but had not been enforced). The Dick Act began the process of standardization and federalization of the volunteer state militia units.[29] To receive federal funds, state militia units were required to meet specific federal standards regarding unit strength, training drills and annual training. For the first time, members of the militia units received federal pay for annual training. Prolonged public debate regarding the military needs of the United States resulted in the 1916 National Defense Act and 1920 amendments which allowed recruitment of a larger standing force, establishment of federal reserve forces, formal re-establishment of the militia as the Army National Guard and increased federal control and fiscal support for the Army National Guard, to include greater responsibilities for federal service.[30] In April 1917, the United States declared war on Germany. In answering the call to federal service, the Army National Guard was to comprise seventeen of the forty-three combat divisions of the World War One American Expeditionary Force (AEF).[31] The Army National Guard Divisions, augmented with draftees and reserve officers, accomplished, among other actions, the piercing of the Hindenburg Line, the crushing of the St. Mihiel Salient and victory in the Meuse-Argonne[32]

During the inter-war years, the National Defense Act of 1933 was passed and further clarified the status of the Army National Guard as a state and federal force.[33] It stipulated that a member of a state Army National Guard was simultaneously a member of the Army National Guard of the United States. This assured the ability of a President to order a mobilization, as would be the case in World War Two.

World War Two began with the German invasion of Poland in September 1939. At this time the Army National Guard included more than 200,000 men comprising eighteen below-strength combat divisions.[34] The Regular Army totaled 190,000 personnel in eleven divisions.[35] Beginning in 1940, and lasting through October 1941, Army National Guard units were mobilized.[36] Many Guardsmen remained on active duty until the end of the war. Half of the eighteen Army National Guard divisions went to Europe, and half to the Pacific.[37] About 75,000 Army National Guard enlisted men became officers during World War Two.[38]

Upon conclusion of the war in 1945, Secretary of War Stimson outlined a new concept of the Army National Guard as a mobilization day force, trained, equipped and immediately available for service in the event of a national emergency.[39] The Army National Guard, of course, retained state responsibilities to protect life, property and public safety. This plan also outlined directions for state and federal responsibilities:

1) States would recruit personnel and furnish armories and storage facilities for the Army National Guard. This was ammended in 1948 it was agreed that the Federal Government would fund 75 percent of armories. [40]

2) The federal government would be responsible for instruction, outdoor training facilities, pay, uniforms, equipment and ammunition. [41]

3) The federal government would provide aid for construction of facilities, something previously done solely by the states.[42]

By the end of 1948, the Army National Guard totaled 5,680 units with an aggregate strength of 682,000 personnel, including twenty-five infantry divisions, two armored divisions, twenty-one infantry-combat teams, twenty-three anti-aircraft battalions and

10

forty-five field artillery battalions. From the time of pre-World War I to this point, the Army National Guard had seen a four-fold increase.[43]

In World War One, the Army National Guard was able to furnish combat divisions. By World War Two the Office of Reserve Components (ORC) had 100,000 officers available to meet the needs of the expanding force structure.[44] In these and other conflicts, the National Guard provided much needed time for the nation to mobilize resources to field a large, trained and well-equipped land force drawn from the larger population. The United States had time and distance from the area of conflict to make orderly preparations for war. Consider, for example, that when Germany invaded Poland in September 1939 the Army consisted of only 187,000 active soldiers, 200,000 National Guardsmen, over 100,000 reserve officers and about 3,000 reserve enlisted Soldiers.[45] It took about two years from initial mobilization to prepare divisions for deployment as part of an Army that would eventually peak at six million personnel.[46]

After World War Two, the Army inherited peacetime overseas missions in Europe and in the Pacific which stretched active component resources. As in past post-war periods, the active component had been maintained at the minimum force structure necessary to meet immediate requirements, and the preparedness of the reserve component was allowed to diminish. It assumed that the nuclear capabilities of the United States would be sufficient deterrent to foreign adventurism. The attack on South Korea in June, 1950 quickly invalidated this assumption as the North Koreans proceeded to defeat allied forces on the peninsula.[47] This may be considered a turning point for the tradition of United States unpreparedness.

In this situation, a combat ready and rapidly deployable reserve component force was needed. However, without sufficient resources to maintain readiness, the Army National Guard was largely unprepared for rapid mobilization and deployment. This, coupled with indecisiveness regarding deployment of these divisions, meant it would take more than one year from mobilization to deploy National Guard divisions to Korea.[48] However, many smaller units deployed in less than six months.[49] All told, about two-thirds of the Army National Guard was pressed into federal service to supplement the needs of the active Army.[50] Eight Army National Guard divisions and many support units were eventually mobilized, equipped, and trained.[51] By early 1951, Army National Guard artillery, engineer and signal battalions were mobilized, brought up to strength deployed and sent into combat in Korea.[52] About one year after mobilization, two divisions were deployed to Europe and two divisions were sent to Japan and then to Korea.[53]

In the period following the Korean War, National Guard elements mobilized on a limited basis on several occasions. President John F. Kennedy declared a mobilization in 1961 in the face of Soviet Premier Khrushchev's threats over the issue of West Berlin.[54] These call-ups served a largely political and symbolic purpose; they were intended to deter war, not fight one. In this sense, Kennedy's plan worked because the Soviets eventually backed down.

The onset of American participation in the Vietnam War marked yet another decisive point in the timeline of the Army National Guard. One key consideration leaders continually face are how the political circumstances and the national mood affect a decision to mobilize the National Guard. When substantial numbers of U.S. troops were first committed to Vietnam in 1965, President Johnson declined to mobilize the

National Guard, electing instead to expand the active duty forces.[55] In his mind, the potential for domestic repercussions precluded a reserve call-up. The impact of this decision on the capability of our Army in Vietnam has been the subject of historical scholarship. For the first time in U.S. history, the citizen-soldier was largely left back at home. However, the unpopularity of the war, the mood of the electorate, and other political consequences for the President were factors which, in addition to the military requirement, affected decisions whether to mobilize. But, by 1968, this situation had changed. Political obstacles remained, but military needs necessitated the use of the citizen-soldier. Eventually, about 20,000 National Guard soldiers mobilized.[56]

The culminating point for active/reserve component integration occurred during Operation Desert Shield/Storm. On November 30, 1990, two Army National Guard mechanized infantry brigades were ordered to active duty in support of Operation Desert Shield and later Operation Desert Storm, the United States effort to defend Saudi Arabia, and, eventually, eject the Iraqi Army from Kuwait and destroy Iraqi military potential[57]. A third Army Guard armored brigade was activated on December 7, 1990.[58] All three brigades were "roundout" units. "Round-out" refers to a program in which one of the three brigades of several active Army divisions is an Army National Guard brigade, not an active Army brigade (there are also a few separate round-out battalions).[59]

Theoretically, an active Army roundout division is brought to full war strength by mobilizing its National Guard roundout brigade. Each of the three brigades activated in late 1990, were designated to join a parent active Army division upon mobilization.

However, the three roundout brigades were not activated until approximately four months after the Iraqi invasion of Kuwait on August 2, 1990, and the beginning of Operation Desert Shield on August 6, 1990.[60] The two that had parent divisions already deployed to Saudi Arabia, and eventually participated in the war against Iraq, did not deploy with those divisions.[61] In the end, none of the three brigades left the U. S. Infact, the only one to be "validated" as combat-ready by active Army trainers was so judged on February 28, 1991 -- the day of the initial cease-fire with Iraq.[62] The experience of these brigades during Desert Shield/Storm generated much criticism and controversy about the viability of the round-out concept as well as the active Army's relationships with the National Guard. The fact that the basic assumption that war-fighting capabilities did not adequately equate with capabilities in EM/DR/SCD has never been seriously re-examined. Moreover, such an assumption has always contained yet another arguable presumption: that war-fighting capability would provide a state Guard with the kinds of personnel and equipment needed for EM/DR/SCD.

Chapter 3

Discussion

"When the three brigades were activated, many soldiers were not completely trained to do their jobs; many noncommissioned officers were not adequately trained in leadership skills...activation of the three round-out brigades also revealed that the post-mobilization training plans prepared by the three brigades during peacetime had underestimated the training that would be necessary for them to be fully combat ready. The plans were based on peacetime evaluation reports that Army officials believed overstated the brigades' proficiency and training readiness. After the brigades were activated, active Army trainers developed substantially revised training plans calling for over three times the number of training days estimated in readiness reports and requiring the support of almost 9,000 active Army trainers and other personnel."[63]

GAO Report (Post Desert Shield/Storm)

Past National Guard mobilizations indicate a force plagued with, unclear missions, lack of equipment and insufficient attention to National Guard-specific needs— overall, a force ill-prepared to be effectively and rapidly utilized as a combat multiplier. The limited nature of immediate threats to the United States early in this century, increased reliance on the deterrent effect of nuclear weapons and a large overseas active duty presence after World War II argued against the need for a full time army in a high state of readiness. It is noteworthy, however, that the need for a more viable National Guard was recognized in 1967 when Public Law 90-168, "Reserve Forces Bill of Rights and Vitalization Act," was enacted.[64] In addition to creating new positions in the Department of Defense (DOD) to oversee the reserve component, the law emphasized the importance of providing the National Guard the wherewithal to satisfy their mobilization readiness requirements. The combined effects of the loss of a credible deterrent use of nuclear weapons, the evolution of sophisticated, highly destructive

15

conventional weapons, as well as the potential for contingency regional conflicts throughout the world, all point to the need for a more ready, rapidly deployable and professional Army National Guard.

The National Guard is a unique military organization with characteristics of the state militias originating in colonial times. Guard units are entities of their respective states under the direction of their governors. According to the Constitution, they can also be called into federal service by the President, thus becoming part of the U.S. Armed Forces under the President's direction. This dual state/federal status has meant that the Guard historically has sought to fulfill two missions that have at times been hard to balance: (1) to serve as the primary combat reserve of the Army and Air Force, and (2) to fulfill a peacetime state mission of ensuring public safety, protecting property and maintaining public order.[65] Under pressures of the Cold War, it was convenient to assume that these two missions were mutually supportive without any additional efforts or arrangements. However, changes in the current U.S. security situation requires a serious re-examination of this assumption. The end of the Cold War, combined with the resultant downsizing of U.S. armed forces, the emergence of a civilian field of emergency management, growing expectations on the part of the public concerning government's ability to respond to EM/DR/SCD and the desire on the part of the President and most governors to meet such expectations demands that such a review address all these potential concerns.[66]

While these forces are trained as well as commanded and controlled by state appointed leaders, funding for these units is provided mainly by Federal allotments. During the mid-1980 Army of Excellence (AOE) restructuring, Army National Guard units were organized and equipped mainly as combat and combat support units.[67]

Historically, this has meant that the preponderance of non-active duty infantry, armor, artillery, attack aviation, military police, and engineer units are found scattered throughout the fifty States in battalion to division size units, with very loose ties to the active forces or themselves. All in all, the Guard's confused involvement in national defense policy and strategy, its role in the U.S. military force structure, its institutional bias for combat roles, and its nearly total reliance on federal funding create a fundamental dilemma for the Guard in its efforts to balance its two missions.[68] "That quandary has made it one of the most problematic of EM/DR/SCD resources, despite its great potential to increase overall capabilities of the nation's emergency management system."[69]

Changes to this structure are the two recently formed Provisional Divisions: the 24th Infantry Mechanized Division at Fort Riley, KS and 7th Light Infantry Division at Fort Carson, CO.[70] The division headquarters is manned by a skeleton force of active duty officers and NCOs with the six Brigade Combat Teams (three in each Division) formed from identified Enhanced Separate Brigades throughout the country. In the same vein, several battalions have attempted to integrate active duty commanders into National Guard units, primarily as commanders. Both attempts are obviously an attempt to increase the integration of the two forces. But have they gone far enough to fix the inherent problems associated with the dual-purpose nature of the National Guard?

An effective methodology for answering this question may be to judge the Guard's current capabilities (based upon historical evidence) against the vision that the CSA has for the Army. While the Guard has not been called upon to deploy as a conventional combat unit since the early 1990's, this information can be deduced from

17

recent experiences at the Army's Combat Training Centers (CTCs). The Combat Training Center Integrated Training Strategy (CTC-ITS), provides battle-focused training for all National Guard units.[71] At least one National Guard Brigade Combat Team has rotated through the CTCs each year for nearly the past decade.[72] Historical experiences and After Action Reviews (AARs) can then be used to project the Guard's actual ability to meet both current and future requirements if they were to be called upon.

Shortcomings exhibited before and during each and every example shown were overcome with added time, emphasis and resources. Herein lies the fundamental problem associated with maintaining the status quo relationship of the National Guard as a reserve combat force to the active duty Army. Given the timeline that the current Chief of Staff of the Army, General Shinseki is attempting to achieve with the reorganization of the active duty forces, the relevance of a slow-to-respond National Guard is clearly in question.

During Desert Shield/Storm, when the National Guard brigades mobilized, brigade commanders were reporting estimates that up to 40 days of post-mobilization training would be needed to be fully combat ready.[73] However, on the basis of their independent assessment of the brigades' proficiency, officials responsible for the post-mobilization training of the three brigades developed training plans calling for over three times the number of days that the readiness reports stated were needed.[74] In a February 1991 report, the GAO reported that the Army's independent assessments of proficiency demonstrated during National Guard units' two-week annual training periods did not provide reliable or useful information to higher commands on the units' proficiency.[75]

Also, the study questioned the validity of National Guard training readiness reports.[76] The GAO made several recommendations to improve the National Guard's training evaluations; however, the Department of Defense said that the Army already had adequate evaluation policies and procedures in place.[77]

This led to the Congressionally mandated AC/RC program where amongst other changes, active duty cadre (Officer and Non-Commissioned Officers) were assigned directly to support the Guard units' training and evaluation.[78] Still, by 1998, the GAO reported that the "...90 days or so of training required to validate the readiness of one brigade may not be a reliable indicator of the time that units will need for future mobilizations because (1) the Army did not specify the criteria to be used in its validation decision and (2) the tremendous amount of active Army resources used to support the brigade's training may not be available in a future crisis."[79] Therefore, both the lead time necessary for adequate train-up and preparation for mobilized Guard units as well as those assets required to meet these demands out of the active duty forces must be seriously reviewed. Given the requirements General Shinseki envisions for the deployment of combat forces into a theater of operation (i.e. one division within four days and five divisions within thirty days)[80], just how relevant of a combat force is the National Guard? Even utilizing the GAO's best case scenario of ninety days post-mobilization train-up, there remains a difference of some sixty days. This delta must be addressed by one of following methods: more time, better training, or refocused missions.

Time Issues

"The only sure deterrent to any potential adversary (who is not insane) in regions of strategic importance to the United States is the certainty of the presence on land, soon after the beginning of any crisis or conflict, of an American ground force large enough to make a quick victory impossible."[81]
Breaking the Phalanx

First, the Army decision-makers could choose to adjust down deployment timetables to meet the much slower reaction time of Guard units. The immediate response envisioned by the CSA would clearly have to be executed by active duty forces conducting rapid deployment contingencies. This would relegate the National Guard to second or third order replacement/augmentation. This is potentially feasible under a two Major Regional Conflict (MRC) scenario which presents the need to delay and "hold" in one theater while simultaneously achieving a rapid victory or "win" in a different theater.[82] However, much discussion has been given to the fact that the National Military Strategy (NMS) will back completely away from the possibility (and therefore the force structure requirement) of such a strategy during the upcoming Quadrennial Defense Review (QDR) in 2001. If infact, the NMS is amended to reflect these opinions, then just what relevance will the National Guard possess if the conflict is over before they are even capable of deploying into theater?

Another aspect of time that must be considered is the ability of the National Guard to achieve and maintain adequate levels of preparation based upon the constraints of their active training schedule. While training for most units is funded for only ten four-day periods and one fourteen period annually, it must be understood that many units and personnel are contributing much more than that. In interviews with division-level staff Guardsmen, most are participating in meetings and training that near ten days per month.[83] This is in addition to their full-time positions in the civilian workplace. To augment them, the Guard has instituted two new programs to infuse full-time members into their ranks.

The ARNG began the Active Component Command/Staff in 1996.[84] This program places active component officer in key Guard positions. They serve in a variety of positions from battalion commander to brigade-level operations and executive officers. While it is too early to observe any effects of this program, both Guard and active duty leaders are optimistic as to the results. In addition, discussions on expanding the program to allow a one-for-one exchange program of battalion-level commanders, executive officers, operations officers, and company commanders are under way.[85]

The second program is the ARNG's Full-Time Support (FTS) program established by Congress to "…organize, administer, recruit, train, and maintain Army National Guard units."[86] The program allows for 45,000 full-time personnel with a budget of $2.8 billion annually.[87] The force currently consists of 23,686 Military Technicians and 22,182 Active Guard Reserve (AGR) soldiers who perform many of the day-to-day operations for the Guard.[88] The majority of FTS personnel, close to 95%, are assigned to or in support of deployable ARNG units.[89] One critique of this program is the fact that the bulk of these personnel were "grown" within the Guard's organization and represent the same deficiencies of understanding and knowledge of Army doctrine, tactics, techniques and procedures (DTTP) as their part-time counterparts.

The fact remains though, that Guard units continually struggle to achieve an adequate level of readiness given the tremendous amount of tasks to be trained in the short periods of time available.[90] Common sense then suggests that either the amount of tasks to be trained must be reduced or the amount of time available to the units must be increased. Given the reality that many of the Guard soldiers maintain full-time jobs in the private sector and are already hard pressed to "squeeze" any more time away from them without jeopardizing their careers, it seems unlikely that anymore available time can be identified. It seems equally unlikely that the tasks needed to be trained can be reduced while maintaining the current status quo within the National Guard's organization and mission. As technology and doctrine continue to evolve in this fast paced environment, it can be assumed that the Guard will continue to lag behind its active duty counterparts. It is inconceivable that they will be able to balance the training of new technologies in addition to fundamental skills, fielding of new equipment and upgrades, and the maintenance of unit readiness without making some fundamental changes.

Training Issues

"The essential characteristics of a good army are that it be well trained and well disciplined. These two characteristics are apparent in every unit achievement, whether in peace or in war. Discipline derives and flows from training and serves to emphasize a fundamental point essential to a philosophy of training: that training is all-encompassing. Training permeates everything a military organization does."[91]

Common Sense Training

Secondly, the Army could institute further changes to the training and preparation of the peacetime National Guard program to attempt to accelerate the post-mobilization requirements. While time has a direct effect on the ability to adequately train, the Guard itself must re-look some of its current training policies. The Army National Guard is attempting to manage and improve overall readiness by prioritizing resources to its units that are designated "First to Deploy".[92] This method of "tiering" ensures that high-priority units receive necessary resources to meet operational readiness requirements and also support the National Military Strategy.[93] Critical units such as Force Support Package (FSP) and the enhanced Separate Brigades have significantly benefited from tiered resourcing, but at the expense of other Guard units.[94]

Lower-priority units such as the eight ARNG Divisions, have struggled to maintain acceptable readiness levels under current fiscal constraints. The Army National Guard is currently working to ensure that all lower-prioritized units are allocated baseline resources, which will allow these units to attain and sustain deployment standards.

23

However, during FY 98, Unit Status Reports (USR) indicated that overall unit readiness levels declined by 5%.[95] Several factors contributed to this decline:[96]

> *Decreased training levels

> *Equipment serviceability

> *Non-duty qualified military occupational specialty (DMOSQ) personnel

And while the CTC-ITS has paved the way for more focused battle-oriented training at the brigade level by scheduling ARNG units into the CTC cycle, the through-put of these units are exceedingly slow by active duty standards. Nearly all active duty brigades will rotate through a CTC annually. Conversely, Guard units culminate their training cycle at a CTC only at the end of an eight-year train-up program.[97] Even then, unit performance is well below that of active duty units.

A review of the past five years' (FY 1996-2000) performance of National Guard brigade combat teams (BCTs) at the National Training Center (NTC) illustrates a disturbing trend. Based upon unit training levels and preparation, scenarios are degraded to meet their lower capabilities.[98] Offensive (meeting engagement) force-on-force missions (normally conducted as close to a one-to-one ratio as possible) are many times reduced to a two- or even three-to-one advantage for the Guard BCTs.[99] Deliberate attacks (doctrinally performed at a three-to-one combat ratio) are routinely conducted instead at a six-to-one ratio in favor of the National Guard BCTs (i.e. a BCT attacking an OPFOR defense consisting of two companies).[100] In addition, the final phase of a normal NTC rotation consists of a transition by the BCT to a live-fire scenario. Commonly referred to as the culmination of a unit's complete train-up cycle, the live-fire phase integrates lessons learned throughout this period as well as those gained during the

24

previous ten days of force-on-force exercise. This phase normally consists of both an offensive and defensive mission against computerized "pop-up" targets. The unit is forced to integrate direct and indirect fires, utilizing live munitions throughout the full spectrum of a BCT's combined arms. For four of the five rotations reviewed, all but one BCT declined to participate in this training. The one unit that did chose to participate, executed only one mission, in a "range-like" scenario which emphasized marksmanship vice maneuver under live-fire conditions.[101]

This does not portray the whole story however. While observations and After Action Reviews (AARs) indicate a general inability of National Guard units to adequately perform at the brigade and battalion levels (as based on published ARTEP standards), small unit performance (i.e. companies and platoons) often met or exceeded those exhibited by their active duty counterparts. Individual and small unit training appears to be achievable given the constraints of time and space the National Guard must deal with. Given the reality of training only four days per month and fourteen days annually, the Guard faces an OPTEMPO problem unlike that of the active duty. Maintaining individual skills and qualifications such as physical fitness, marksmanship, And MOS-specific training, leaves little time or resources available for unit-level training. When faced with the reality of needing to train subordinate units (squads, platoons, companies) prior to proceeding to higher ones(battalions, brigades), there is insufficient time to reach the BCT level. In addition, most of these skills are degradable over time, thereby forcing units to re-train these tasks annually, not allowing for progression to the next unit level of training. Given these realities, it is easy to see how even an eight-year training program would not enable a BCT to reach an adequate level of readiness.

Adding to the proficiency of Guard small unit performance is the reduction of personnel turbulence as compared to their active duty counterparts.[102] Due in part to much longer crew and small unit stability, these Guard units build the type of cohesion and standard operating procedures that is only achieved over time. While most active duty units strive but usually fail to maintain stability within crews and units of between six and twelve months, Guard units normally maintain stability nearing the three to five year mark.[103] Instead of attempting to correct a problem that is confined by time and training realities, Army leaders should look at ways to accentuate the positive aspects of the current Guard, to include small unit proficiency.

Relevance of National Guard Combat Forces

A third option Army leaders today could choose is the reallocation of forces between the ARNG and the Army Reserve. Today, the ARNG is chiefly a combat force whereas the Army Reserve is mainly a support force.[104] Anticipating the future international climate, compounded by the pressures of reducing the defense budget, the force structure of the U.S. Armed Forces is not only likely to retain a force mix, but one with an increased emphasis on reserve component forces. In the case of the U.S. Army, National Guard forces will be heavily relied upon to both augment the active duty forces as necessary. These forces will be called upon to act independently in certain situations in order to allow the active duty to maintain all of its current (and projected future) commitments while simultaneously stabilizing and presumably reducing, unit OPTEMPO. The issue then, is how best to integrate these assets into both the active duty Army and maximize their capabilities while also minimizing their limitations.

Understanding the historical heraldry of state militias and their evolution to modern day Guard units is essential to being sensitive to the dual nature of today's Army National Guard missions. While several studies have been conducted concerning the "warrior ethos" and the esprit de corps that promotes within today's Guardsmen, emphasis must be placed on the best integration of these forces into current Army strategy. Why then, in the twenty-first century, would U.S. state governors need the type and organization of forces currently allocated? Take for instance the state of Rhode Island. The National Guard units found there include self-propelled artillery, infantry, air defense and armor units to name a few. What is the "threat" to Rhode Island that the

Governor would/has activated his units? Most agree that these missions would include assistance to state citizens during heavy winter storms, hurricane relief, and crowd control. Then why would the Governor need to employ long range (20+ kilometer), precise, lethal indirect fires as those offered by his self-propelled howitzers? Is it not more likely that he could need the potential for engineers, medics, civil affairs, transportation, military police, etc. type units in future anticipated state disasters? If so, by restructuring the Army National Guard units in this way, the Governor would possess the proper tools to respond to relevant situations within his locality.

Might it be possible to organize and equip state National Guard units that are capable of providing the type of support their governors are likely to need while also contributing to the assumption of active federal duty demands? Obviously, many of the issues aforementioned would be identical if equipment and missions were shifted between Guard and Army Reserve forces to include levels of proficiency and time constraints. But by shifting many of the support functions to the state Guard units, they can maintain the ability to support active duty forces as required while simultaneously providing more relevant assets to their state leaders.

What is it then that governors need to provide support to their local population? Leaders must be willing to re-look the organization and focus of the state National Guard units. It is obvious that these states no longer need the types of units found in their present day arsenal for the kinds of operations they do and will perform in the future. By identifying these types of units/capabilities and organizing them into highly deployable and useful force "packages", the dual nature of National Guard units may dissipate.

Chapter 4

Recommendations

"The Department of Defense (DoD) should give systematic consideration to the needs of states' Guard units in EM/DR/SCD during its force structuring and budget processes and in decisions on basing assets. Additionally, the transfer of CS and CSS assets to the Guard should be continued. An advisory panel with membership from among ihe parties at interest warrants consideration. FEMA should make state integration of Guard resources into state emergency plans an important agenda item in the development of its Performance Partnership Agreements."[105]

National Academy of Public Administration
(Report to Congress—1998)

It has become fairly evident that given the vision of future combat operations combined with the problems associated with the dual-missions the National Guard faces today, that a change is in order. Indeed, the Guard Bureau, in conjunction with the Army, have investigated the possibility of restructuring the organization in the past. In 1996, the Secretary of the Army approved the Army National Guard Division Redesign Study (ADRS) plan.[106] This plan called for the conversion of up to twelve Guard combat brigades and slice elements to combat support and service/support (CS/CSS) units between FY 99-12.[107] For example, the state of Michigan, will inactivate the 3-126 Infantry Battalion and activate a Supply and Service Battalion Headquarters, a Combat Heavy Equipment Transport Company, a Water Purification Detachment, and a Fire Fighting Team.[108] This process has not only been embraced by both the Army and the State Guard units identified for conversion, but has actually been accelerated to be complete by FY 05.[109]

29

Therefore, given that the concept of converting combat units to appropriate CS/CSS units appears to be acceptable to all sides, the only remaining issue then is to what extent this conversion will take place. The time is right to align this decision with the radical changes taking place in the active duty force today. In order to satisfy both the States' and Federal requirements placed upon the Guard, a total reorganization and re-focusing of priorities in necessary. By doing so along the lines of CS/CSS conversion, the National Guard would possess the assets needed to function effectively at both levels. In addition, they could leverage this force structure to not only increase their relevance in the future, but also, to achieve a long desired aspiration. This change would offer the National Guard the ability to demand a commensurate portion of the defense budget (replete with the authority to control it themselves), reduce the perception of active versus reserve component rivalries, as well as introduce the possibility of a unified command of their own (a four star position that could be called the United States Command/USCOM).

First, by converting existing combat units to organic CS/CSS organizations, the Guard would offer better capabilities to their respective states. Governors would organically possess those types of units necessary to deal with common "threats" to their states commonly known as emergency management response. The Federal Emergency Management Agency (FEMA), whose responsibility it is to coordinate State response in conjunction with federal assets to such operations acknowledges this point. In a study to Congress and FEMA, the National Academy of Public Administration states that the attributes that make military organizations valuable in EM/DR/SCD go beyond the specific logistical capabilities that these organizations happen to possess.[110] In short, the basic characteristics of effective military organizations are precisely the characteristics that are called for in situations of emergency, disaster, or civil unrest. The study suggests

specific examples of military units' value in this type of operation that include the

following potential:[111]

1) Military organizations are well-organized and highly disciplined bodies of

persons that are designed to cohere in situations of stress, confusion, and crisis

when other organizations may unravel or experience loss of mission capability. At

the minimum, they represent large bodies of "disciplined hands and feet" that can

be set to any pressing task such as debris removal, sandbagging, or securing and guarding

an area.

2) Military organizations possess durable systems of command, control, and

communication that are not easily disrupted or degraded by chaotic situations, austere

conditions, changes in personnel, or physical and psychological stress.

3) Military units have greater logistical capabilities than most of their civilian

counterparts. To some extent, all military units, even noncombatant units, have the

quality that the military calls "combat maneuver": the ability to rapidly assemble,

mobilize, transport, and deploy large bodies of personnel and equipment across great

distances.

4) Military members are conditioned to endure hardship, discomfort, and danger

without allowing these conditions to degrade individual and organizational effectiveness

and mission performance.

5) Military equipment, is designed for high durability and possesses "off-road"

capabilities that can be useful in emergencies. Examples include Humvees, short takeoff

and landing transport aircraft (C-130 Hercules), vertical takeoff and landing or rotary wing aircraft (HU-1 Huey helicopters), reverse osmosis water purification units (ROPUS), heavy-lift cargo helicopters (CH-47 Chinooks), field medical and surgical hospitals (MASH units), electric generators, halogen field lights, meals ready to eat (MREs), and many other items.

6) Military organizations have the capacity, even in times of stress and confusion, for the disciplined application of force - including deadly force under constitutionally prescribed conditions - to ensure that the law is upheld and that lives and property are protected

7) Military organizations are able to operate in the field for prolonged periods under difficult conditions without relying on normal civil infrastructure such as roads, sewers, water, utilities, transportation, or food distribution systems.

8) Military organizations have the capacity to provide for large numbers of civilian personnel under austere conditions; for example, they are proficient in mass feeding and sheltering, and in the provision of sanitation and medical care in the field.

9) As the embodiment of the state's power, military organizations possess potent symbolism, which can be either positive or negative. In situations of crisis and its aftermath, this symbolism can be powerfully positive. The use of military units symbolizes the government's commitment - and therefore the mutual commitment among citizens - to succor those in dire need, and to maintain law and order.

Secondly, the conversion of these units could provide the type of specificity needed to assure direct budgeting to the National Guard Bureau, rather than through the oversight of the Department of the Army. Missions like riot control, natural and manmade disasters as well as unconventional homeland defense such as Nuclear, Biological, and Chemical attack response, could provide a specific expertise to the National Guard that would not directly compete with active duty Army budgeting dollars.

The system currently in place illustrates the lack of timely federal response to local situations. Once disaster strikes, prompt aid for victims is among the most politically popular causes, turning even budget conservatives into free spenders. Federal funds cannot be released until a state requests them, and the President officially declares a "disaster area".[112] President Bush ran afoul of public opinion when torrential floods hit the Southeastern U.S. states in the fall of 1993.[113] The former President failed to immediately declare the area as official disaster areas, even though in retrospect, the delay was more likely the effect of late requests by the states' Governors. This lesson however, seems not to have been lost on President Clinton, as he regularly makes disaster declarations. In fact, sometimes even preceding the disaster as was the case with Hurricane Floyd.[114] On average, President Clinton has declared approximately 45 disasters each year of his presidency, up from 25 per year in the 1980s.[115] Throughout the 1990s, Congress has approved an average of $3.7 billion a year in supplemental disaster aid compared to less than $1 billion a year in the 1980s (these figures are time adjusted).[116] The public expects fast money and quick help when a disaster occurs and there is no reason to believe they will expect less because the problem may be larger or more serious in scope.

On a recent, albeit, more limited scale, recent National Guard efforts to prepare for catastrophic terrorist incidents seem to be a step in the right direction. As a result of a Presidential Decision Directive (PDD) on terrorism, the National Guard has a Military

Support Detachment Rapid Assessment Initial Detection or MSD (RAID) unit established in each of the 10 regions of the Federal Emergency Management Agency (FEMA).[117] These units consist of full time Guard members who must report to the Armory within one hour of notification.[118] They would provide the Incident Commander the capability to detect radiological, chemical, and biological agents using the same state of the art detection gear (though not combat "hardened") available to the Marine Chemical and Biological Incident Response Force and the Army Technical Escort Unit.[119] They also will possess a unified mobile command suite with redundant communications and its own power source.[120] Although not intended for independent deployment overseas, it is conceivable, they could rapidly respond to assist forward support forces or friendly states as needed.[121]

Thirdly, these National Guard units would be capable of offering relief to active duty units in those types of international commitments that do not necessarily call for combat units. Recent Humanitarian Relief Operations offer the perfect example of this type of employment. Not only have these missions been cited as some of the reasons for active duty decline in combat readiness[122], but have also arguably, poorly executed by these same units at the outset. By having appropriately trained personnel and units familiar with this type of operation available to Army leaders, the opportunity for successful execution of this type of mission increases. In addition, these types of units primarily operate at the Battalion level and below. This would complement their strength of small unit performance and would most likely build upon experience and training gained in their civilian occupations. For the most part, these types of specialties (i.e.

medical, military police, engineering, etc.) are filled by personnel who possess formal training and/or job experience of the same type in their civilian occupation.[123] Therefore, advances in their specific fields as well as overall training/readiness would be met by day-by-day exposure to their occupations. In addition, military training would introduce new workers into the civilian market with requisite skills to be utilized by them. As organic units used to operating together and who possess established command and control headquarters tailored to these types of operations, planning for and deploying these units is simplified. Rather than the ad hoc method of selecting units throughout not just the active and reserve components, but also within different regions of the country, planners could identify complete and organic units for deployment.

Lastly, in the wake of a potential National Missile Defense program, the Army could project the National Guard as a logical owner/operator of this system. Doing so would garner the support of the State Legislators where the system is employed. This addition would not only enhance the Army's influence in Department of Defense decisions, but also lend credibility to an Army-controlled unified command---the United States Command. This concept has been suggested by many who believe given the existing and future threat to homeland security, a unified commander (CINC) should be designated to prepare for and direct defense issues. This idea would serve both the Army and the National Guard well. The Army could gain yet another CINC position while more importantly, the Army National Guard could achieve a long-time goal—a four-star position within its ranks.

Counter-Arguments

Such a proposed change of this magnitude produces many dissenting opinions and concerns. These issues include: reluctance by both the Army Reserve and the National Guard to alter their traditional roles and organizations, States' fear of over-utilization of its assets for Humanitarian Operations, as well as the overall reduction of combat reserve forces that would result from such a proposition.[124] While this list is not all-inclusive, these issues can be considered both the most likely to arise and the most serious threat to future changes.

The reserve component, especially the National Guard possesses great political and popular support within their states.[125] Any changes that would ultimately affect the Guard must receive the support of its political and uniformed leaders. As with any situation, change is typically viewed as negative until the positives of the plan can be explained. It would take the consensus of Army leaders, elected Federal and State officials as well as the understanding of the civilian populations to make these changes possible. First, the Army must clearly articulate the effect that numerous Humanitarian Operations are having on the combat capabilities of its active duty forces. The "can-do" attitude of senior leaders in the past is admirable but detrimental to potential progress. While normally seen as a weakness to admit an assigned mission or task is unachievable or harmful, the Army's leaders must take an honest review the facts, and candidly assess the situation at hand. What they will find is two-fold: 1) combat units may not be the best suited/prepared units to execute these types of operations and 2) the price of skill-degradation of these units may be slowly deteriorating the Army's ability to effectively

36

conduct combat operations in the future. With findings like these, the decision to alter the status quo becomes obvious and imperative. In short, by identifying a critical shortfall in national defense, the cries for change will surely follow.

Secondly, the fear of Guard over-utilization is a legitimate concern. Clearly, over-use of Armed forces in general over the past eight years has been an ongoing issue for the Army's senior leadership. Exit interviews of junior enlisted personnel and officers has shown that the increased OPTEMPO experienced in the Army is a major contributing factor to their departure.[126] A change to National Guard force structure and mission focus may then possibly result in the greatest unforeseen benefit of all. By maintaining the preponderance of this type of capability within the Guard, Federal decision-makers will be forced to be more selective and articulate on its decisions to deploy U.S. forces to this type of operations. No longer will the President and the National Security Council have the ability to commit U.S. forces into potentially long-term and dangerous missions without first obtaining the approval of the states' officials where the units will come from. While this alone may not prevent or limit U.S. involvement in these operations, it surely will illustrate the need for Federal leaders to better assess and analyze the situation before committing U.S. assets.

In addition, while over-all OPTEMPO of Army forces may not decrease, there will be a much larger pool of units available to use for these missions. With all fifty states possessing generally similar types of units, capable of commitment to these types of missions, the ability to spread the workload around the whole Guard increases. This presents the opportunity to actually reduce OPTEMPO to those few units who in the past have been routinely performing such operations, by providing the Army and National leadership with the increased options that a more relevant National Guard provides.

Lastly, it must be clearly understood that such a radical change within the Army National Guard forces has to be accompanied by similar changes within the Army Reserve structure. The Army still needs to have a combat reserve force in the chance of prolonged conventional warfare. The combination of both the lack of a peer military competitor over the next ten-to-twenty years, and U.S. propensity to conduct missions in a both a joint and combined environment, decreases the need to possess large numbers of combat forces in the reserve components. The deficiencies illustrated by the National Guard in the past can be assumed to continue if these responsibilities were simply shifted to the Army Reserve. Therefore, the same recommendations of organizing these units at the Battalion and below level would allow for the ability to augment active duty forces in both a timely and effective method. In addition, given Army Reserve units are federal assets, devoid of the dual-mission pitfalls associated with the Guard, these forces provide greater flexibility of scheduling for training, equipping, and relocation within the U.S.

Chapter 5

Conclusion

"We must judge our national security strategy by its success in meeting the fundamental purposes set out in the preamble to the Constitution, '... provide for the common defence, promote the general Welfare, and secure the Blessings of Liberty to ourselves and our Posterity....' Since the founding of the nation, certain requirements have remained constant. We must protect the lives and personal safety of Americans, both at home and abroad. We must maintain the sovereignty, political freedom and independence of the United States, with its values, institutions and territory intact. And, we must promote for the well being and prosperity of the nation and its people."[127]

U.S. National Security Strategy
(October 1998)

If the United States Army is to maintain land dominance in the future, it must think boldly and act boldly now. We cannot afford to defer research, development, or fielding of new systems capable of leveraging our technological advancements. The active duty force must be the nation's global "911" force. It must be capable of rapidly projecting combat power, quickly winning a major theater conflict, and then turn this re-shaped theater over to the reserve component for post-conflict stability and support operations (SASO). Upon completing this transition, the active component must immediately be prepared and postured to fight another major theater conflict.

The Army National Guard must organize, train, and prepare to handle all domestic and international humanitarian and disaster relief operations. It must be capable of augmenting other federal agencies for anti-drug and anti-terrorist efforts. It must be capable of satisfying requirements for long-term international peacekeeping operations. And finally (and most importantly), it must execute these missions with little to no active

39

duty support.

As shown, a humanitarian relief model (which mirrors those types of units needed in the event of a domestic crisis) makes perfect sense for all involved. States would have readily available and trained units available to conduct relevant missions in support of its citizens. In addition, the Army would have ready-made humanitarian support packages available for deployment to external national areas (i.e. Haiti, Somalia, etc.). An unforeseen benefit may be the insistence of State Governors demands on the NCA prior to the Federalization of their units for a mission deployment. This may infact, take away some of the indiscriminate power exhibited by recent administrations to deploy U.S. troops into such operations, and return it to the Congress (as expressed in the Constitution). In addition, these types of units operate at a lower or more decentralized level (i.e. MP battalions versus brigades or divisions) and fit perfectly into the current National Guard training strengths. Due to limitations in training time and areas, most National Guard units exhibit strong platoon and company level skills and weak to non-existent brigade and above attributes. Why not build and re-organize the National Guard along its strengths instead of continuously attempting to alter its weaknesses? Overall, this approach represents a win-win situation for all involved.

An Army with these capabilities will be able to execute peace keeping and other MOOTW operations without degrading its ability to execute two nearly simultaneous (or overlapping) major theater wars as part of the joint service team. Fixing shape, respond, and prepare responsibilities allows each component of the Total Army to build on their traditional strengths. It allows for a smaller, capable projection force while attempting to reduce the burden of funding on the American taxpayer. The solution is clear. Our citizen-soldiers must take care of the home-front and shape the international security environment in order to allow the active force to focus on responding to the full spectrum of crises when called to do so. By doing this, the Total Army can prepare now to meet the challenges of an uncertain future. The Army's AC/RC integration program during the early 1990s was named "Bold Shift"[128]…it is time once again for the Army to make a bold shift towards the future.

APPENDIX A

Guard Involvement in EM/DR/SCD
(The Use of the National Guard in Support of Civilian Authorities)[129]

Natural Disasters

**Hurricane Andrew, Florida, 1992

More than 6,000 Florida Army National Guard troops and 1,350 Louisiana National Guard troops were mobilized in response to the damage done by Hurricane Andrew.' The 160 mph winds destroyed more than 85,000 homes, and damage estimates ranged between $15 billion and $20 billion. The devastation left in Andrew's path prompted the largest Guard call-up in Florida's history: Gov. Lawton Chiles activated more than 6,100 Army Guard members and more than 230 Air Guard members during the first week of the disaster. A tent city was erected to shelter the more than 230,000 people that were homeless, without food, water, and electricity in a 165 square-mile area as a result of the storm. In addition to tactical law enforcement, the guard was asked to perform missions including food and water distribution, search and rescue missions, and transportation of supplies for relief efforts; additional duties included the clearing of debris from streets using chain saws and heavy machinery, and the medical treatment of the injured in migrant camps. During the first week of response, Guard personnel r distributed more than 200,000 meals-ready-to-eat (MREs), and 6000 people lined up for food at one Guard food distribution point at a peak time. By the time the cleanup was completed, some Guard personnel were on duty for an entire year.

**Mississippi River Flooding, Midwest, 1993

As a result of unusually heavy rains during spring and summer of 1993, record setting flooding occurred along the Mississippi and Illinois rivers resulting in over $12 billion in property, crops, and personal loss. Over 10,000 Guardsmen and women, representing the nine midwest states affected (Illinois, Iowa, Kansas, Minnesota, Missouri Nebraska, North Dakota, South Dakota and Wisconsin), were called into service performing duties such as security, levee maintenance and sandbagging, medical support, aviation support, and water distribution. In addition to the thousands of Guardsmen and women building up levees and transporting relief supplies, specialized units (i.e. water purification units) were deployed from neighboring states to affected areas.

42

**Tropical Storm Alberto, July, 1994

The severe rains caused by Tropical Storm Alberto caused the worst flooding in Georgia history when rain fell at a mind-numbing rate of up to 20 inches in less than 24 hours. Rivers, streams, and other waterways surged over their banks and flooded substantial portions of Georgia, Alabama, and Florida. The worst damage occurred in central and southern Georgia when the Ocumlgee and Flint Rivers burst their banks. Georgia National Guard personnel performed many tasks, including law enforcement, water distribution, sandbagging around a hospital threatened by rising water from the Flint River, delivering food, water and other critical supplies, bridge construction, and road repair. Overall, 2.3 million gallons of bottled water were distributed; 4.8 million gallons of water produced by reverse osmosis purification units (ROPU); 3.1 million gallons of water distributed by water trailer; over 154,000 meals served; over 1,000 hours of flight time log in response to the disaster; 184 patients transported by Medivac helicopters; more than I million vehicle miles driven; and at peak strength, 3,683 Guard members, nearly one-third of the entire Georgia National Guard were on state active duty. In Florida over 600 Guard personnel performed similar missions, including establishment of a hot shower facilities, and flights to carry badly needed food and medicine to people stranded by the rising water.

In Alabama, Guard engineering personnel worked to maintain a levee in Elba's downtown district which was threatened by flooding. Alabama guard personnel also provided more than 800,000 gallons of potable water in Macon, Georgia, making good use of the previous year's experience performing a similar mission in Des Moines, Iowa during the midwest floods of 1993.

Civil Disturbances

**Homestead Works, Carnegie Steel Corporation, 1892

A strike was called at the Homestead works of the Carnegie Steel Corporation in support of an eight hour working day and the entire Pennsylvania Guard, 8,000 men, were called out by the governor as soon as the strike began. Full mobilization took only thirty-two hours, but it continued in effect for seventeen days. In fact, selected units remained on duty for three months. The intervention of the Guard was costly for the times, with expenses running as high as a million dollars. Though the intervention can be credited with minimizing bloodshed, the maintenance of order by the troops vitiated the strike and left laborers with a strong distaste and distrust for the Guard.

Phenix City, Alabama, 1954

On July 22,1954,Alabama Governor Gordon Persons dispatched the Guard under MG Walter J. Hanna to Phenix City and neighboring Russell County in response to the murder of a respected local leader who was shot down three days before he was to testify before a grand jury on the county's high crime rate and vote fraud. Gen. Hanna immediately read the Governor's proclamation from the courthouse steps, relieved the Sheriff of his duties and replaced him with LTC Jack Warren and 10 armed Guardsmen. This procedure was repeated with the Chief of Police. In short order, Phenix City and surrounding Russell County were under the control of Gen. Hanna and the Alabama National Guard. Gen. Hanna carefully handpicked officers and soldiers with backgrounds in law enforcement, or with experience as investigators, street police, or lawyers, and set about to "clean up the mess." By early 1955 the "cleanup" was complete with approximately $ 5 million in illegal gambling equipment confiscated. More importantly, the first clean, fair election in years was held. The Guard's occupation came to an end on January 17,1955.

Los Angeles, 1992, Urban Riot

More than 10,000 Army National Guard and 1300 Air National Guard troops were called for riot control duty in the Guard's first civil disturbance response in a major American city since the days of anti-Vietnam War protests. Tasks included patrolling and securing areas as assigned by the Los Angeles Police Department (LAPD) during sixteen hour shifts. Despite widely criticized delays in deployment, observers generally credited the presence of the Guard with providing an authoritative and reassuring presence that was instrumental in restoring order.

<u>Man-Made Emergencies</u>

Oklahoma City Bombing, 1995

Over 375 members of the Oklahoma Guard assisted in the aftermath of the April 19, 1995 bomb explosion at the Alfred P. Murrah Federal Building in Oklahoma City. The Army and Air Guards handled duties including security, searching for victims and helping with the crush of the media. Among the first on the scene were 100 military police guarding the 15-square block area cordoned off just after the explosion. Ten members of the 245th Medical Co. worked at a temporary morgue downtown or at the Medical Examiner's Office processing bodies and gathering evidence. Also assisting in security were 34 Air Guard security police from bases in Tulsa and Oklahoma City and a UH-1 helicopter crew.

**Other examples of manmade emergencies are dam failure, hazardous material accidents or dumping, nuclear powerplant incidents, etc.

Appendix B

GUARD RESPONSE EXAMPLES[130]

The following is a partial list showing examples of Guard response to natural disasters, civil disturbances, and manmade emergencies.

Natural Disasters

*New England Blizzard, 1977

*California-San Francisco earthquake, 1990

*Hurricane Andrew, Florida, 1992

*West Virginia Fire, 1992

*Hurricane Iniki, Hawaii, 1992

*Idaho Fire, 1992

*Mississippi River Flood Mid-west states, 1993

*Northridge Earthquake, Los Angeles, California, 1994

*Tropical Storm Alberto, GA, AL, & FL, 1994

*Long Island New York fire, 1995

Civil Disturbances

*Carnegie Steel Corporation strike, Homestead works, 1892

*Pullman sleeping Car Company strike, Chicago, 1894

* Phenix City, Alabama, martial law, 1954

*Arkansas, Little Rock, school integration,1957

*Oxford, Mississippi,1962

*Tuscaloosa, Alabama, 1963

*Selma, Alabama, 1965

*Chicago, Illinois, Democratic National Convention, 1968

*San Francisco State, student riots, 1968

*Detroit, Michigan Riots, 1968

*Jackson State, Mississippi student riots, 1970

*Postal strike, 1970

*Ohio, Kent State student riots, 1971

*Rhode Island, hospital workers strike, 1989

*California, Rodney King trial, Los Angeles, 1992

Man-Made Emergencies

*Oklahoma City Bombing, 1995

Endnotes

[1] Samuel P. Huntington, *The Soldier and the State,* (Cambridge, Massachusetts: The Belknap Press of Harvard University Press, 1957), 401.

[2] United States Joint Chiefs of Staff, *"Joint Vision 2010"*, (Washington, D.C.: Office of the Joint Chiefs of Staff, 1996).

[3] Martin Binkin and William W. Kaufmann, *U.S. Army Guard & Reserve: Rhetoric, Realities, Risks*, (Washington, D.C.: The Brookings Institution, 1989), 4.

[4] Ibid., 11.

[5] Advisory Commission on Intergovernmental Relations, *The National Guard: Defending the Nation and the States*, (Washington, D.C.: ACIR, 1993), 8.

[6] *National Military Strategy of the United States of America*, September 1997, 1.

[7] Robert Kagan, "The Benevolent Empire," *Strategy and Force Planning, 3rd Edition*, (Newport, Rhode Island: Naval War College Press), 178.

[8] United States Joint Chiefs of Staff.

[9] Dubik, MG James, "ICBT at Fort Lewis", *Military Review*, (Fort Leavenworth, KS: Sep/Oct 2000), 18.

[10] Bennie J. Wilson III, *The Guard and Reserve in the Total Force*, (Washington, D.C.: SSR Incorporated, 1985), 25.

[11] National Academy of Public Administration, *The Role of the National Guard in Emergency Preparedness and Response*, (Washington, D.C.: NAPA, 1997), xi.

[12] General Accounting Office, *Disaster Management: Improving the Nation's Response to Catastrophic Disasters*, (Washington, D.C.: GAO, 1993).

[13] Ibid., 11.

[14] Ronald E. Sortor, *Army Active/Reserve Mix*, (Santa Monica, CA: RAND, 1998), 9.

[15] Ibid., 21.

[16] MG (R) William A. Navas, Jr., "Posse comitatus, the Army of the 21st Century and the law of unintended consequences," *National Guard*, (Washington, D.C.: 1999).

[17] *The Constitution of the United States*, Article I, Section 8.

[18] Association of the United States Army (AUSA), *The Active And Reserve Components: Partners In The Total Army*, (Arlington, VA: AUSA, 1990), 6.

[19] Advisory Commission on Intergovernmental Relations,7.

[20] Bennie J. Wilson III, 14.

[21] Martin Binkin and William W. Kaufmann, 38.

[22] Association of the United States Army (AUSA), 6.

[23] Ibid., 6.

[24] Ibid., 7.

[25] Martin Binkin and William W. Kaufmann, 13.

[26] Ibid., 8.

[27] Bennie J. Wilson III, 14

[28] Martin Binkin and William W. Kaufmann, 36.

[29] Bennie J. Wilson III, 31.

[30] Martin Binkin and William W. Kaufmann, 44.

[31] Robert K. Wright and Renee Hylton-Greene, *A Brief History of the Militia and the National Guard*, (Washington, D.C.: National Guard Bureau, 1986), 9.

[32] Ibid., 11.

[33] Bennie J. Wilson III, 33.

[34] Ibid., 35.

[35] Martin Binkin and William W. Kaufmann, 38.

[36] Ibid., 39.

[37] Bennie J. Wilson III, 36.

[38] Martin Binkin and William W. Kaufmann, 39.

[39] Bennie J. Wilson III, 44.

[40] Martin Binkin and William W. Kaufmann, 41.

[41] Bennie J. Wilson III, 46.

[42] Robert K. Wright and Renee Hylton-Greene, 13.

[43] Ibid., 18.

[44] Martin Binkin and William W. Kaufmann, 49.

[45] Robert K. Wright and Renee Hylton-Greene, 15.

[46] Ibid.,16.

[47] Martin Binkin and William W. Kaufmann, 52.

[48] Ibid., 63.

[49] Ibid.

[50] Ibid., 66.

[51] Robert K. Wright and Renee Hylton-Greene, 18.

[52] Ibid., 21.

[53] T.R. Fehrenbach, *This Kind of War*, (Washington, D.C.: Brassey, 1963), 111.

[54] Robert K. Wright and Renee Hylton-Greene, 22.

[55] Ronald H. Spector, *The Early Years—The U.S. Army in Vietnam*, (Washington D.C.: Center of Military History, 1985), 105.

[56] Ibid., 107.

[57] Robert L. Goldich, The Army's Roundout Concept After the Persian Gulf War, (Washington, D.C.: Congressional Research Service, 1991), 7.

[58] Ibid., 8.

[59] The Army defines "round-out" units as reserve component units "designated to raise understructured Active Component divisions to standard mobilization deployment configurations." National Guard Bureau Information Paper. *SUBJECT: Affiliation Program.* May 1, 1981.

[60] Ibid.

[61] Ibid.

[62] United States General Accounting Office, *Peacetime Training Did Not Adequately Prepare Combat Brigades for Gulf War*, (Washington, D.C.: GAO, 1991), 12.

[63] Ibid., 13.

[64] Robert L. Goldich, 23.

[65] Robert K. Wright and Renee Hylton-Greene, 32.

[66] National Academy of Public Administration, 3.

[67] Robert K. Wright and Renee Hylton-Greene., 26.

[68] Robert K. Wright and Renee Hylton-Greene, 17.

[69] National Academy of Public Administration, xii.

[70] Speech, BG Taguba, Active Duty Advisor (AC/RC), Region V, 15 MAY 99, National Training Center, Fort Irwin, CA.

[71] National Guard Bureau, *Annual Review of the Chief*, (Fiscal Year 1998), 28.

[72] Ibid.

[73] GAO, *Peacetime Training Did Not Adequately Prepare Combat Brigades for Gulf War,* 12.

[74] Ibid.

[75] Ibid., 13.

[76] Ibid. 14.

[77] Ibid.

[78] Ibid., 15.

[79] Ibid.

[80] Dubik, MG James, 21.

[81] Douglas A. Macgregor, *Breaking the Phalanx*, (Westport, CT: Praeger Publishers, 1997), 225.

[82] *National Military Strategy of the United States of America*, September 1997.

[83] Personal Interviews Conducted October 2000 with Colonel Sullivan, Edward S., Senior Army Advisor, California Army National Guard; Colonel Van Goor, Jacob A., Chief of Staff, 40th Infantry Division (Mechanized); Major Willand, Bernd, Assistant to the Chief of Staff, 40th Infantry Division (Mechanized).

[84] National Guard Bureau, *Annual Review of the Chief*, (Fiscal Year 1998), 36.

[85] Ibid.

[86] Ibid.

[87] Ibid., 38.

[88] Ibid.

[89] Ibid.

[90] Personal Interview Conducted October 2000 with Colonel Van Goor, Jacob A., Chief of Staff, 40th Infantry Division (Mechanized).

[91] LTG(R) Arthur S. Collins, *Common Sense Training*, (Novato, CA: Presidio Press, 1978), 1.

[92] National Guard Bureau, 30.

[93] Ibid.

[94] Ibid.

[95] Ibid., 31.

[96] Ibid., 28.

[97] Ibid., 29.

[98] Author's personal observations and recollections of four National Guard rotations (FY 1996-1999) and interviews of Observer/Controllers during the fifth (FY 2000)

[99] Ibid.

[100] Ibid.

[101] Ibid.

[102] Personal Interview Conducted October 2000 with Colonel Van Goor, Jacob A., Chief of Staff, 40th Infantry Division (Mechanized).

[103] Ibid.

[104] Martin Binkin and William W. Kaufmann, 13.

[105] National Academy of Public Administration, 5.

[106] National Guard Bureau, 36.

[107] Ibid., 39.

[108] Ibid.

[109] Ibid., 41.

[110] National Academy of Public Administration, 9.

[111] Ibid., 10.

[112] Ibid., 12.

[113] Ibid., 14.

[114] Ibid., 21.

[115] General Accounting Office, 17.

[116] Ibid.

[117] National Academy of Public Administration, 87.

[118] National Guard Bureau, 33.

[119] National Academy of Public Administration, 114.

[120] Ibid., 113.

[121] Ibid.

[122] Taw, Jennifer M., Persselin, David and Leed, Maren, *Meeting Peace Operations While Maintaining MTW Readiness,* (Santa Monica, CA: RAND's Arroyo Center, 1998), 32.

[123] Association of the United States Army (AUSA), 37.

[124] Personal Interviews Conducted October 2000 with Colonel Sullivan, Edward S., Senior Army Advisor, California Army National Guard; Colonel Van Goor, Jacob A., Chief of Staff, 40th Infantry Division (Mechanized); Major Willand, Bernd, Assistant to the Chief of Staff, 40th Infantry Division (Mechanized).

[125] Robert K. Wright and Renee Hylton-Greene, 3.

[126] Ibid., 111.

[127] The White House, *A National Security Strategy For A New Century*, (1998).

[128] Robert K. Wright and Renee Hylton-Greene, 32.

[129] National Academy of Public Administration, 123.

[130] Ibid., 126.

BIBLIOGRAPHY

Military Monographs/Thesis

Breitling G. "The Army Reserve: Relevant in Force XXI?" Army War College, Carlisle Barracks, PA, 15 April 1997.

Carlow, L. "Restructuring the Army National Guard Combat Divisions: Issues and Implications." Army War College, Carlisle Barracks, PA, 15 April 1996.

Fraley, J. Jr. "The Army Reserve Role in Military Support to Civil Authorities: A New Approach for the 21st Century." Army War College, Carlisle Barracks, PA, 1998.

Harrel J. "A United Army for the 21st Century." Army War College, Carlisle Barracks, PA, 31 May 1997.

Heller, C.E. "Twenty-First Century Force: A Federal Army and a Militia." Army War College Studies Institute, Carlisle Barracks, PA, May 1993.

MacIntyre, Jon Paul G. "Army Reserve Component Restructure: Does the Canadian Model Have Validity for U.S. Army Reserve Components?" Master of Military Art and Science Thesis, Fort Leavenworth, KS, 1997.

Newcomb, C. L. "Principles of Future Army Force Structure Design." Army War College, Carlisle Barracks, PA, 20 April 1993.

Payne H. "The United States Army Reserve: A Relevant Force for the Twenty-First Century?" Army War College, Carlisle Barracks, PA, April 1997.

Quan, A. "The Effectiveness of Army National Guard Combat Units for Major Regional Conflicts: Perception or Reality?" Army War College, Carlisle Barracks, PA, 15 April 1996.

Robbs, C. "The 'Just-in-Time' Force for the Army." Army War College, Carlisle Barracks, PA, 30 April 1997.

Government Commissions and Reports

Department of the Army. *One Team, One Fight, One Future, Total Army Integration.* Washington, D.C., 1998.

General Accounting Office. *Disaster Management: Improving the Nation's Response to Catastrophic Disasters*, GAO/RCED-93-186. Washington, 1993.

Minister of National Defence and Veterans Affairs. Department of National Defence. *The Special Commission on the Restructuring of the Reserves Report*. Ottawa, Canada, 30 October 1995.

President of the United States. Office of the Secretary of Defense. *Reserve Component Programs (Fiscal Year 1998 Report of the Reserve Forces Policy Board)*. Washington, D.C., March 1998.

Secretary of the Army. United States General Accounting Office. *Force Structure: Army National Guard Divisions Could Augment Wartime Support Capability*. Washington, D.C., March 1995.

Secretary of the Army. United States General Accounting Office. *National Guard: Peacetime Training Did Not Adequately Prepare Combat Brigades for Gulf War*. Washington, D.C., September 1991.

Secretaries of the Army and Air Force. National Guard Bureau. *1998 Annual Review of the Chief (National Guard Bureau)*. Washington, D.C., 1998.

Secretary of Defense. National Defense Panel Report. *Transforming Defense: National Security in the 21st Century*. Washington, D.C., December 1997.

Taw, Jennifer M., Persselin, David and Leed, Maren. RAND's Arroyo Center. *Meeting Peace Operations While Maintaining MTW Readiness*. Santa Monica, CA, 1998.

United States Army. Office, Chief Army Reserve. *United States Army Reserve Long Range Plan (1993-2023)*. Washington, D.C., Summer 1993.

U.S. Congress. Congressional Budget Office. *Structuring the Active and Reserve Army for the 21st Century*. Washington, D.C., December 1997.

U.S. Congress. Congressional Research Service. *The Army's Roundout Concept After the Persian Gulf War*. Washington, D.C., 22 October 1991.

U.S. Congress and Federal Emergency Management Agency. National Academy of Public Administration. *The Role of the National Guard in Emergency Preparedness and Response*. Washington, D.C., January 1997.

U.S. Congressional Requesters. United States General Accounting Office. *Army Reserve Components: Cost, Readiness, and Personnel Implications of Restructuring Agreement*. Washington, D.C., March 1995.

U.S. Senate. United States General Accounting Office. *DOD Reserve Components: Issues Pertaining to Readiness*. Washington, D.C., 21 March 1996.

Newspaper and Magazine Articles

Associated Press. "Avoiding Contact", *Dallas Morning News*, 4 August 2000.

Carpenter, Jasper and Freddie R. Waggoner, "Leading the National Guard into the 21st Century", *Field Artillery*, Issue 3, pages 34-37, May/June 1998.

Dubik, MG James, "ICBT at Fort Lewis", *Military Review*, Issue 5, pages 17-23, Sep/Oct 2000.

Earhart, Douglas B., "AC/ARNG Integrated Division for the 21st Century", *Field Artillery*, Issue 3, pages 42-44, May/June 1998.

Meyers, Steven Lee. "Army Weighs An Expanded Role For National Guard Combat Units", *New York Times*, 4 August 2000.

Peters, Katherine McIntire, "On Guard", *Government Executive*, Volume 30, pages 34-37, January 1998.

Plewes, Thomas J., "Army Reserve Vision", *The Officer*, Volume 76, Issue3, pages 29-31, April 2000.

Plewes, Thomas J., "Reserve is Indispensable for 21st Century Army", *The Officer*, Volume 76, Issue1, pages 44-47, January/February 2000.

Plewes, Thomas J. MG, "The Army Reserve's Vision for the 21st Century", *Army Reserve Magazine*, Volume 45, Issue 3, pages 4-29, Spring 2000.

Reimer, Dennis J.; Thomas J. Plewes, and Roger C. Schultz. "Taking the Total Army Idea into the Next Century", *The Officer*, Volume 74, Issue 9, pages 29-31, October 1998.

Veronee, Bernard F., Jr., "Army National Guard Division Redesign", *Army Logistician*,

Books and Other Reference Material

Fehrenbach, T.R., *This Kind of War*, NewYork: The Macmillan Company, 1963.

Collins, Arthur S., LTG, *Common Sense Training*, California: Presidio Press, 1987.

Macgregor, Douglas A, *Breaking the Phalanx*, Connecticut: Praeger Publishers,1997.

McMaster, H.R., *Dereliction of Duty*, New York: HarperCollins Publishers Inc., 1997.

Spector, Ronald H., *The Early Years—The U.S. Army in Vietnam*, Washington D.C.: Center of Military History, 1985.

United States Joint Chiefs of Staff, *"Joint Vision 2010"*, Washington, D.C.: Office of the Joint Chiefs of Staff, 1996.

Wright, Robert K. and Hylton-Greene, Renee, *"A Brief History of the Militia and the National Guard"*, Washington, D.C.: National Guard Bureau, 1986.

<u>Personal Interviews</u>

Colonel Sullivan, Edward S., Senior Army Advisor, California Army National Guard.

Colonel Van Goor, Jacob A., Chief of Staff, 40th Infantry Division (Mechanized).

Major Willand, Bernd, Assistant to the Chief of Staff, 40th Infantry Division (Mechanized).